I am a Koala

Heather Kissock

Go to **www.av2books.com**, and enter this book's unique code.

BOOK CODE

T726927

AV² by Weigl brings you media enhanced books that support active learning.

AV² provides enriched content that supplements and complements this book. Weigl's AV² books strive to create inspired learning and engage young minds in a total learning experience.

Your AV² Media Enhanced books come alive with...

Audio
Listen to sections of the book read aloud.

Video
Watch informative video clips.

Embedded Weblinks
Gain additional information for research.

Try This!
Complete activities and hands-on experiments.

Key Words
Study vocabulary, and complete a matching word activity.

Quizzes
Test your knowledge.

Slide Show
View images and captions, and prepare a presentation.

... and much, much more!

Published by AV² by Weigl
350 5th Avenue, 59th Floor New York, NY 10118
Website: www.av2books.com

Copyright ©2017 AV² by Weigl
All rights reserved. No part of this publication may be reproduced, stored in a retrieval system, or transmitted in any form or by any means, electronic, mechanical, photocopying, recording, or otherwise, without the prior written permission of the publisher.

Library of Congress Cataloging-in-Publication Data
Names: Kissock, Heather.
Title: Koala
Description: New York, NY : AV2 by Weigl, 2017. l Series: I am l Includes bibliographical references and index.
Identifiers: LCCN 2015037940l ISBN 9781489641137 (hard cover : alk. paper) l
  ISBN 9781489641144 (soft cover : alk. paper) l ISBN 9781489641151
  (single-user ebook : alk. paper) l ISBN 9781489641168 (multi-user ebook :
  alk. paper)
Subjects: LCSH: Koala--Juvenile literature.
Classification: LCC QL737.M384 K57 2015 l DDC 599.2/5--dc23
LC record available at http://lccn.loc.gov/2015037940

Printed in the United States of America in Brainerd, Minnesota
1 2 3 4 5 6 7 8 9 0 19 18 17 16 15

102015
151015

Editor: Heather Kissock   Art Director: Terry Paulhus

The publisher acknowledges Getty Images, Corbis, Minden Pictures, Alamy, iStock, and Shutterstock as the primary image suppliers for this title.

I am a Koala

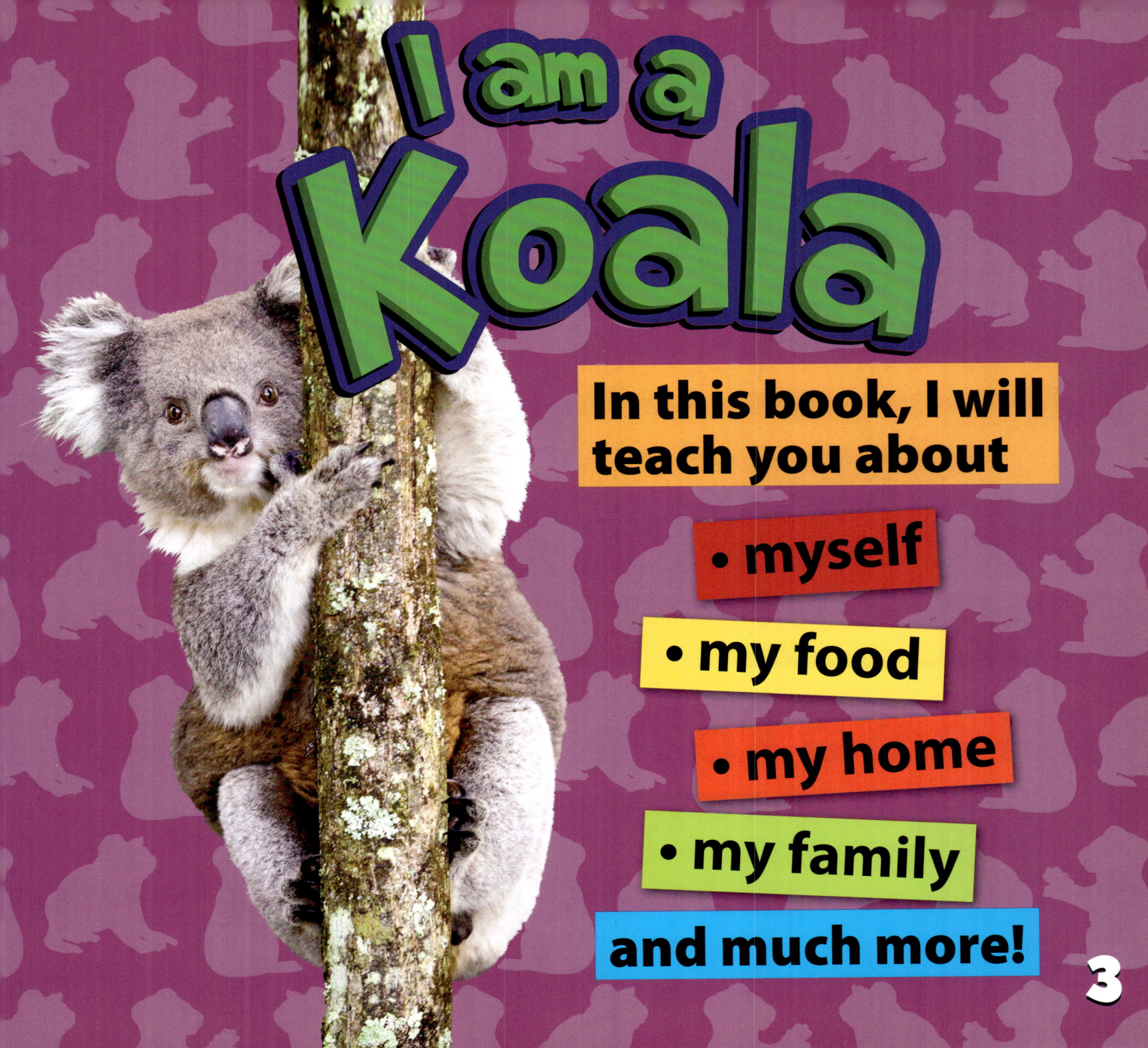

In this book, I will teach you about

- myself
- my food
- my home
- my family

and much more!

I am a koala.

I grow up in my mother's pouch.

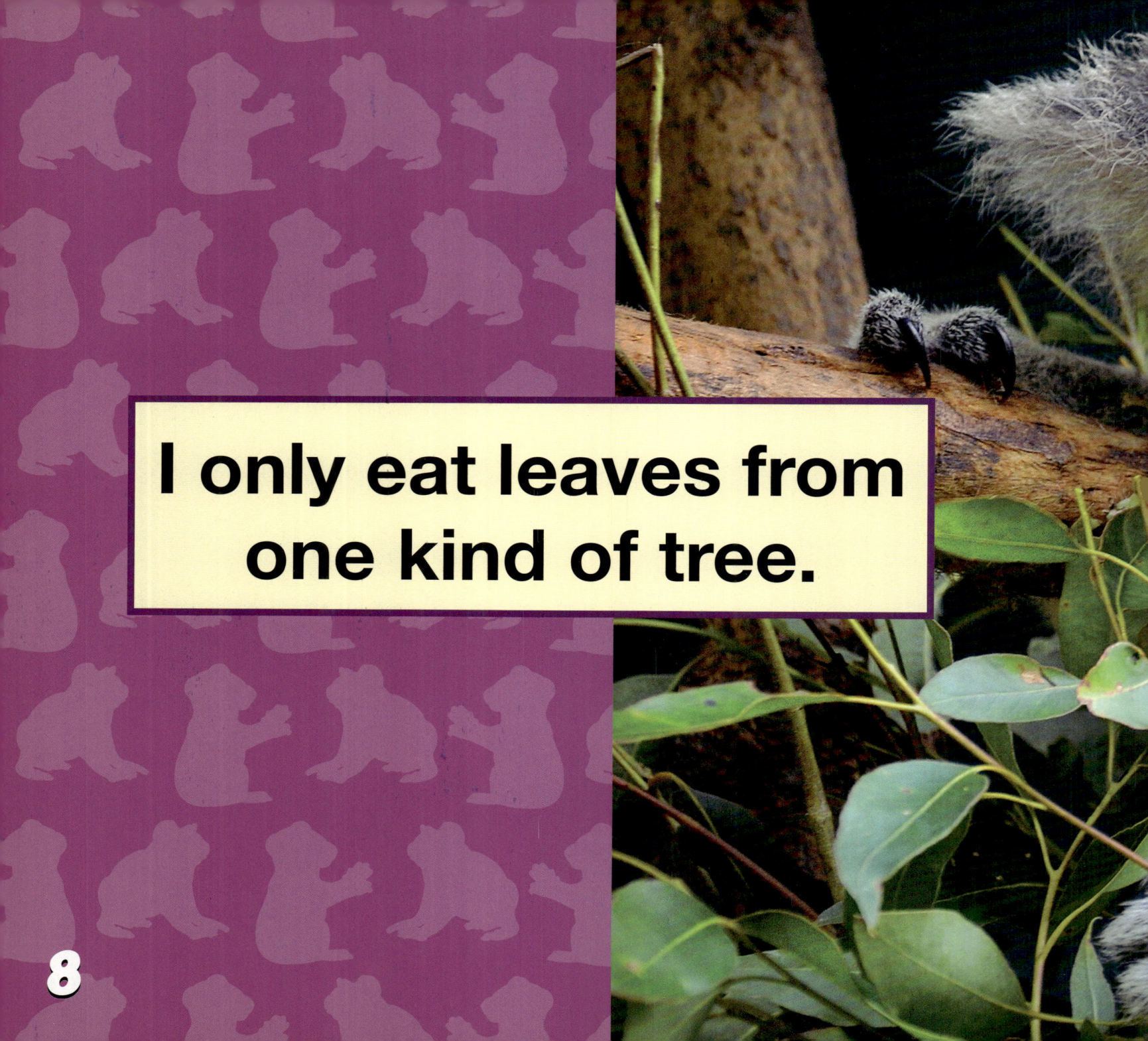

I only eat leaves from one kind of tree.

I have two thumbs on each hand.

I sleep for up to 20 hours each day.

I like to be alone.

I can sound like a motorcycle when I talk.

17

I smell like a cough candy.

I live in the forests of Australia.

I am a koala.

KOALA FACTS

These pages provide detailed information that expands on the interesting facts found in the book. They are intended to be used by adults as a learning support to help young readers round out their knowledge of each amazing animal featured in the *I Am* series.

Pages 4–5

I am a koala. Koalas are often referred to as koala bears. However, the koala is not a bear. Instead, a koala is a type of marsupial. These are animals best known for carrying their babies in a pouch located on their body. Marsupials are mammals. This means that they are warm-blooded, give birth to live young, and feed their young milk.

Pages 6–7

I grow up in my mother's pouch. Baby koalas are called joeys. The size of a jelly bean at birth, joeys are born hairless and cannot see or hear. A joey will spend about 6 months in the pouch developing. At that point, the joey begins to travel out of the pouch to find food.

Pages 8–9

I only eat leaves from one kind of tree. Eucalyptus trees serve as a koala's home and food source, with the trees' leaves filling the koala's dietary needs. Koalas live in the crooks of the tree's branches and come to the ground only to move from one tree to another. Eucalyptus leaves are toxic to most animals, but koalas have special bacteria in their digestive system that overcomes the effect of the toxins.

Pages 10–11

I have two thumbs on each hand. Both of the koala's thumbs are opposable. This means they can wrap around tree branches. The large gap between the thumbs and fingers allows the koala to maintain a strong grip on branches and to effectively pick leaves from the tree.

Pages 12–13

I sleep for up to 20 hours a day. A koala can eat more than 2 pounds (1 kilogram) of leaves per day. Besides being toxic, the leaves are also very fibrous and provide little in the way of nutrition. Koalas need their sleep time to digest their food and to conserve their energy. Koalas are active mainly at night.

Pages 14–15

I like to be alone. Koalas are mainly solitary animals that only come together to mate. A koala's home range consists of a cluster of trees, which it visits regularly. Several koalas may live in the same area, but each usually keeps to its own trees within that area.

Pages 16–17

I can sound like a motorcycle when I talk. Although generally quiet animals, koalas can produce a variety of sounds. Their loud bellowing is comparable to a motorcycle revving and is believed to indicate dominance. Koalas sometimes let out loud screams when under stress. Mothers use hums, clicks, and grunts to communicate with their young.

Pages 18–19

I smell like a cough candy. Eucalyptus oil is used in cough medicines to calm throat inflammation. Due to the amount of eucalyptus leaves a koala eats in a day, the animal can sometimes give off a slight eucalyptus odor. Adult males tend to emit a musky smell. This smell comes from a scent gland located in a bald patch on their chests. Males rub this gland on trees to mark their territory.

Pages 20–21

I live in the forests of Australia. Habitat loss is the main issue facing koalas. The forests they live in are being cleared to make room for residential and business development. Forest fires also destroy their habitat. Recent estimates put the current population at less than 80,000.

KEY WORDS

Research has shown that as much as 65 percent of all written material published in English is made up of 300 words. These 300 words cannot be taught using pictures or learned by sounding them out. They must be recognized by sight. This book contains 32 common sight words to help young readers improve their reading fluency and comprehension. This book also teaches young readers several important content words, such as proper nouns. These words are paired with pictures to aid in learning and improve understanding.

Page	Sight Words First Appearance
4	a, am, I
6	grow, in, mother, my, up
8	eat, from, kind, leaves, of, one, only, tree
10	each, hand, have, on, two
12	day, for, to
14	be, like
16	can, sound, talk, when
20	live, the

Page	Content Words First Appearance
4	koala
6	pouch
10	thumbs
16	motorcycle
18	cough candy
20	Australia, forests

Check out av2books.com for activities, videos, audio clips, and more!

 Go to av2books.com

 Enter book code T726927

 Explore your koala book!

www.av2books.com